LIFE IN THE MILITARY

LIFE IN THE
US NAVY

by Emma Huddleston

BrightPoint Press

San Diego, CA

BrightPoint Press

© 2021 BrightPoint Press
an imprint of ReferencePoint Press, Inc.
Printed in the United States

For more information, contact:
BrightPoint Press
PO Box 27779
San Diego, CA 92198
www.BrightPointPress.com

LIBRARY OF CONGRESS CATALOGING-IN-PUBLICATION DATA

Names: Huddleston, Emma, author.
Title: Life in the US Navy / Emma Huddleston.
Description: San Diego : ReferencePoint Press, 2021. | Series: Life in the military | Includes
    bibliographical references and index. | Audience: Grades 10-12
Identifiers: LCCN 2020002454 (print) | LCCN 2020002455 (eBook) | ISBN 9781682829776
    (hardcover) | ISBN 9781682829783 (eBook)
Subjects: LCSH: United States. Navy--Juvenile literature.
Classification: LCC VA58.4 .H83 2021 (print) | LCC VA58.4 (eBook) | DDC 359.1/20973--
    dc23
LC record available at https://lccn.loc.gov/2020002454
LC eBook record available at https://lccn.loc.gov/2020002455

CONTENTS

AT A GLANCE

- The US Navy mainly protects the United States at sea. It is the world's most powerful navy.

- There are six branches in the US military. The US Navy is one of the branches.

- The process of joining the navy is called enlisting. People talk to recruiters. They must pass medical and background checks. They go through special training called boot camp.

- Boot camp lasts seven to nine weeks for enlisted sailors. It can take up to thirteen weeks for officers.

- Many people in the US Navy work on ships. Some jobs include flying planes, repairing machines, and working in health care.

- Life on a ship is broken up into shifts. Different areas of the ship are made for work, enjoyment, and rest. People get used to sharing space and being out at sea.

- The navy sends some people overseas to serve. This process is called deployment. It often lasts six to nine months.

- Some people are active duty. They work full-time in the navy. Others join the US Navy Reserve. They work part-time. Civilians also work for the navy. As of 2020, the US Navy had 339,094 active duty members and 103,395 reserve members. The navy employed 282,121 civilians in that year.

DEFENDING THE COUNTRY

B rie Coger yells, "Fire in the hole!" She presses a button on a remote. An explosion happens in another area. The ground shakes. Coger and her team have destroyed a dangerous explosive.

Coger is an officer in the US Navy. She works as an Explosive **Ordnance** Disposal (EOD) Technician. Her job is to find and

Safely disposing of explosives is one of many important jobs in the US Navy.

get rid of explosives. She keeps US troops

and **civilians** safe. She says, "I believe in

creating a world better than I found it. I think

that's what's given me the drive to make it

in Navy EOD."[1]

Explosives can be anywhere. Some are even underwater. Sometimes Coger must dive into the ocean to deal with these explosives. She may have to dive up to 300 feet (90 m). She must wear special protective gear. She may have to walk into dangerous areas on land. For Coger, life as an EOD officer is exciting. Her team is ready to help at all times.

THE WORLD'S LARGEST NAVY

The US Navy is a branch of the US military. The United States has the most powerful navy in the world. It is responsible for areas all over the globe. It has ships in the Pacific,

The US Navy's ships represent the United States across the globe.

Atlantic, and Indian Oceans. US Navy ships

are also in the Mediterranean Sea, Persian

Gulf, and Arabian Sea. About one hundred

navy ships are out at sea on any given day.

It takes many people doing a variety of jobs to keep the US Navy running smoothly.

Naval ships range in size. Smaller ships sail near coastlines. These ships may be used to help people after a natural disaster. For example, navy sailors may help people recover after a flood. Larger ships travel at sea for long periods of time. Some can launch **missiles**. The US Navy also uses airplanes. Planes can land on and take off from some ships.

The US Navy helps people every day. Its main job is to defend the United States. Navy sailors protect the country from enemies at sea. The navy also keeps shipping routes open. Sailors represent their country in the world's oceans.

CHAPTER ONE

HOW DO PEOPLE JOIN THE NAVY?

The process of joining the US Navy is called enlisting. There are many steps in the process. People first talk to a recruiter. The recruiters work for the US Navy. They answer questions and give more information about life in the navy. They guide people through the application process. They also help people find jobs.

A navy recruiter trains other recruiters.

Recruiters explain the benefits of joining. Some benefits include the opportunity to travel and learn new skills. People who enlist can also get money for education and health care. Thomas Schwab joined the navy for these reasons. He said, "During [the] time while I was homeless, I decided to enlist in the United States Navy. . . . It was the choice that would give me a free education. It would give me a foundation to build the rest of my life on."[2]

TYPES OF SERVICE

After meeting with a recruiter, people decide when to enlist. They can enlist and start serving in the navy right after high school. They may enlist early but finish college before serving.

People also decide whether to serve full- or part-time. Full-time service is called active duty. Another option is the US Navy Reserve. Reserve positions are part-time.

But people in the reserve may be called to serve full-time during a war or other type of emergency. They are always trained and ready.

Many people apply to be enlisted sailors. Others join as officers. Enlisted sailors make up about 83 percent of the people in the navy. They carry out missions at

WHAT ARE THE CHALLENGES?

A career in the military can be rewarding. But it does come with challenges. Navy sailors might be away from loved ones for a long time. They may also have to risk their lives on certain missions. Some people may find it hard to commit to many years of service. People must weigh the pros and cons to see if the navy is the right fit for them.

A US Navy captain arrives on a ship. Captains are navy officers.

sea. Officers oversee sailors. They tell

sailors what to do. They plan and organize

the missions.

ENLISTING

People who decide to enlist are called

recruits. They must meet age requirements.

Enlisted sailors must be between the

ages of seventeen and thirty-nine. Seventeen-year-olds need a parent's permission to enlist. Officer recruits must be at least nineteen years old. Officers have different focuses, or specialties. The maximum age requirement depends on the specialty. Most require officers to be less than forty-two years old.

There are education requirements for recruits. Enlisted sailors must have completed high school or passed a test showing they have high-school level skills. Officers must have a four-year college degree.

There are additional requirements. Active-duty recruits must prove they are able to serve full-time. They cannot have serious financial troubles or family responsibilities. These things could take them away from their job. The US Navy also does not allow these recruits to use drugs or alcohol. Everyone takes a urine test. Sometimes people in the navy are randomly tested. The tests show if anyone breaks these rules.

After people decide how they want to serve, they apply. They fill out an application form. Then they go to a Military Entrance

Navy recruits line up at a Military Entrance Processing Station.

Processing Station (MEPS). There are many

of these stations throughout the country.

Recruits finish the enlistment process

at a MEPS. Doctors check the health

of the recruits. Recruits also go through

a background check. Then they take

a special exam. It is called the Armed

Services Vocational Aptitude Battery

(ASVAB) test. The ASVAB assesses their skills and passions. It helps recruits see which navy jobs would be a good fit for them. They must score at least a thirty-five on the ASVAB to get into the navy.

The final step is the **oath** of enlistment. All military recruits must take this oath. They promise to defend the United States.

TRAINING

After recruits take the oath, they start a training program. This program is called basic training or boot camp. Enlisted recruits train for seven to nine weeks.

They go to the Great Lakes Naval Training Center in Illinois.

Instructors shout orders at recruits throughout boot camp. The instructors are navy officers. Recruits must obey them. Recruits go through physical training. They also take classes. They learn the navy's

THE CREATION OF THE NAVY

The US Navy was created on October 13, 1775. The Revolutionary War (1775–1783) had recently begun. Great Britain had colonies in North America. British leaders ruled these colonies. Many colonists opposed British rule. They wanted to be independent. They fought the British. Great Britain lies across the Atlantic Ocean. Some battles were fought at sea. The colonists needed a navy for that reason.

Navy recruits march at boot camp in Illinois.

core values. These values are honor,

courage, and commitment.

Much of navy boot camp happens in

classrooms or indoors. This setting helps

prepare recruits to work on ships. Ships

have many tight indoor spaces.

Each week of boot camp has a different

focus. For example, the focus in week three

is hands-on training. Recruits board a ship. They practice first aid and flag signaling. Flag signaling is a type of code. It helps ships communicate without radio. Sailors wave flags with certain colors, numbers, and images. These flags represent secret messages.

Recruits practice shooting guns in the fourth week of boot camp. They choose a career path in week five. The US Navy offers a variety of job options. Recruits talk with officers to learn more about these jobs. Personality and skill tests can help recruits find the right job for them. For example, one type of job is a chaplain. A chaplain is a religious leader. One navy chaplain says, "It's a lifestyle of sacrifice and hard work, but you get to be with people."[3]

Recruits go through the Navy Physical Fitness Assessment (PFA) while in boot camp. The PFA has three parts. The first part is a medical screening. Doctors check recruits for health issues. They look for issues that would make recruits unable to serve. Then the recruits' body measurements are taken. Their heights and weights are checked. The third part of the PFA is the Physical Readiness Test (PRT).

Members of the navy continue Physical Readiness Tests throughout their time in the navy.

It includes strength and stamina testing.

The passing scores depend on a recruit's

gender and age.

Boot camp is not the only time people

in the navy go through the PFA. The PFA is

done twice each year. This continues for as long as someone is in the navy.

OFFICER RECRUITS

Officer recruits go through different training programs. Some go to Officer Candidate School (OCS). The navy's OCS is at Naval Station Newport. This naval base is in Newport, Rhode Island. The OCS course lasts thirteen weeks. Other recruits go to Officer Development School (ODS). This school is also in Newport. The ODS program takes five weeks. It prepares recruits to become higher-ranking officers.

Officers go through physical training.

They also learn how to lead others.

Sometimes they learn skills for their specific

career path.

THE NAVAL RESERVE OFFICERS TRAINING CORPS

College students can train to become naval officers. They go through the Naval Reserve Officers Training Corps (NROTC). More than 160 schools offer this program. The navy pays up to $180,000 for each person's education. NROTC students learn leadership skills. They do community service projects. The NROTC program also offers summer training. Students can work on board naval ships. They may travel and work with other countries' navies. They become officers when they graduate from college.

CHAPTER TWO

WHAT JOBS ARE AVAILABLE?

People in the US Navy have many career choices. Some people become sailors. Technology and engineering jobs are available too. Civil engineers help construct buildings and other structures. Mechanics take apart engines and repair machines. The navy also hires computer experts. These people are called

Computers are an important part of the modern navy.

Information Systems Technicians (ITs). They keep communication systems working. They may also intercept messages sent by enemy forces. Enemy forces might send coded messages. The US Navy can read the messages to learn an enemy's secrets.

Support jobs are also important. For example, the navy hires nurses and doctors. They help and support other people in the navy. They care for people who are injured or ill. Lieutenant Ashley Flynn is a nurse in the navy. She mostly worked in hospitals. Then she was **deployed** to Djibouti, Africa. Her deployment lasted eight months.

NAVY EDUCATIONAL PROGRAMS

The US Navy offers programs to help people pay for college. Sometimes the navy helps pay for people's textbooks and housing too. In exchange, students agree to serve in the navy after graduation. The navy has programs for students interested in nursing, engineering, and nuclear power.

She says, "I have really lived out my life and my years and gotten the most out of it."[4] She continued working as a nurse in the navy after deployment. She helps manage and train other nurses.

Many navy jobs require specialized training. Recruits might need to go to an "A" school. They do this after boot camp. "A" schools teach them the skills they need for their jobs. For example, recruits who want to become ITs must go to an "A" school. The school is in Pensacola, Florida. The training takes about twenty-four weeks.

Recruits learn about computer networks and communications systems.

NAVY PILOTS AND NUKES

In addition to ships, the navy also uses aircraft. The navy has special ships called aircraft carriers. These ships are large. Some are more than 1,090 feet (330 m) long. They rise high above the water. They have runways on their decks. Pilots can land aircraft on these runways. Planes can also take off from them. Taking off from or landing on a ship is difficult. The runway has limited space. It is usually only 500 feet (150 m) long.

Landing on an aircraft carrier is a challenge. It takes a skilled pilot and crew to do it safely.

All navy pilots are officers. People must enlist as an officer to become a pilot. They go to OCS. Then they take a training course at the Naval Aviation Schools Command. This school is in Pensacola. The training course takes six weeks. Then people go through flight training. They learn how to navigate and use aircraft.

Another job that requires special training is a navy nuke. Navy nukes work with nuclear reactors. Nuclear reactors power navy submarines. They also power some navy ships. The fuel inside a nuclear reactor is called uranium. In the reactor, uranium atoms are split. This process releases a lot of energy. This energy can power a ship for a long time. Gasoline and other types of fuel do not last as long. Nuclear power is a better option for long missions.

Ships in the Navy

Aircraft carrier

In 2019, the US Navy had ten aircraft carriers. More than 4,000 people work on each aircraft carrier.

Cruiser

Cruisers are mainly used for warfare. They are usually armed with missiles.

Submarine

In 2019, the US Navy had seventy-two submarines.

Amphibious ship

These ships help move large equipment from sea to land. They also help during coastal battles.

The US Navy has a wide variety of ships with different missions.

Navy nukes take care of nuclear power systems on board. There are three main nuke jobs. Some people are machinist's mates. They maintain the reactor and other machines. They make sure all the parts are working. Electrician's mates also work with the machines. They can solve electrical problems. Other people work as electronic technician's mates. They know how the whole system works together. People in these three jobs have similar tasks on non-nuclear ships.

Navy nukes go through three levels of training. They first go through boot camp. Then they go to an "A" school. Finally, they go to the Naval Nuclear Power School. This school is in Charleston, South Carolina. Recruits learn more about nuclear systems.

Working with a nuclear reactor requires a lot of special equipment and training.

UNIQUE JOBS IN THE NAVY

The US Navy has many types of missions.

Navy teams may need to capture an enemy.

Or they may need to rescue **hostages**.

Navy Sea, Air, and Land Teams (SEALs)

are used for these secret missions. SEAL

Teams are special fighting forces. They are trained to carry out missions in all types of environments. They sneak up on the enemy at night. They prepare and plan for missions during the day. They practice entering and exiting areas from the sea, air, and land.

Some navy missions involve submarines. Submarines are underwater ships. The navy may use them to sneak up on an enemy. Submarines patrol in the ocean. They are equipped with underwater missiles called torpedoes. Another type of submarine is a rescue vehicle. It can rescue other submarines in the event of an accident.

People are needed to operate submarines. These people are called submariners. Sailors must volunteer to work on submarines. They prepare to spend long periods of time underwater. Submariners have challenging jobs. Space is limited. There may be more than one hundred submariners on board.

WHAT IS LIFE LIKE ON A SUBMARINE?

Submariners are sent out on missions for three to six months. They often stay underwater for more than a month at a time. In that time, they do not see the sun. They have two six-hour work shifts each day. They have six hours of free time. Then they have six hours to sleep. There are often not enough beds. People must sleep in shifts.

Submarine crews work in tight quarters.

The navy also helps with rescue

missions. People may need saving after

floods or other natural disasters. Members

of the military might need help too. A

pilot could be stranded at sea if her plane

crashes in the ocean. Navy divers help

rescue these people. A navy ship might take a diver to the rescue spot. Or a diver might be lowered into the water from a navy helicopter. Divers must be strong swimmers. They might have to swim against waves or currents.

Divers also do a variety of other tasks. They patch holes in ships. They search for sunken objects such as planes or ships. They dive all around the world. One navy diver says, "What pushes me about this community is the people. . . . That has definitely been the biggest motivation for me."[5]

Becoming a Navy SEAL involves underwater training.

People find the right job by combining their interests and skills. Some jobs require more education or training after boot camp. Sometimes more physical tests are also needed. Navy SEALs, divers, and EOD teams must do extra fitness tests. Navy SEALs recruits go through the Basic Underwater Demolition/SEAL (BUD/S) program. This training happens in Coronado, California. It takes six months.

BUD/S is challenging. The recruits do timed runs on the beach. They swim in the ocean. They climb ropes. They practice parachuting from aircraft. Recruits must meet physical requirements. They have to do one hundred push-ups in two minutes. They must do one hundred sit-ups in two minutes. One week of BUD/S is particularly tough. Recruits get just four hours of sleep

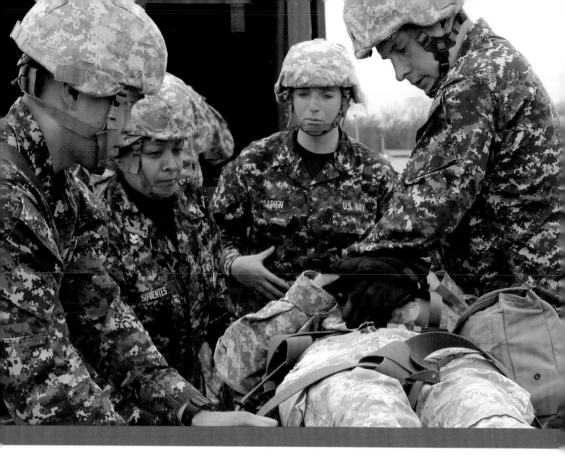

US Navy Reserve sailors participate in a medical training exercise.

each night. They do a lot of running and

other physical activities.

HOW LONG IS THE COMMITMENT?

Navy recruits must commit to serve

a certain number of years. The time

commitment depends on many factors.
Enlisted sailors usually commit to serving
for four years. Sailors with additional training
and officers may commit to more time.
Sailors who take part in navy education
programs may have to commit to serve
longer. The navy pays for their schooling.
In exchange, it requires them to serve
more years.

People in the US Navy Reserve must
serve at least two years. They must do drills
for sixteen hours each month. Drills are
training exercises related to their jobs. This
training is flexible. People can fit it into their

own schedules. They can split their time over multiple weekends or weekdays. Or they can complete all sixteen hours of drills in one weekend.

In addition, people in the reserve must do two weeks of training each year. They might go to other parts of the United States to train. Or they might train in another country. They usually train in teams. They have assigned groups.

There are many job opportunities in the reserve. For example, people can work in health care or construction. Reserve careers are flexible. People may have a

Members of the navy take an oath when they become officers.

civilian job while they are in the reserve. Or

they may go to college.

RATINGS, RATES, AND RANKS

Each navy job has a rating. A badge shows

a person's rating. A rating is a combination

of letters and numbers. For example, cooks

in the navy are called culinary specialists. Their rating is "CS."

Enlisted members of the navy also have rates. A rate shows how senior a person is. Rates start at E-1. They go up to E-9. E-1 sailors are often called seamen. Those in the middle rates are called petty officers. Those in the top rates are called chief petty officers. An E-9 is a master chief petty officer (MCPO).

Officers have ranks. Their ranks start at O-1. They go up to O-10. An O-1 is called an ensign. An O-5 is a captain, and an O-10 is an admiral.

The top-ranked MCPO is known as the master chief petty officer of the navy.

Promotions happen when empty spots need to be filled. The navy can hire a certain number of people for each position. There are fewer people at each level as rates or ranks increase. For example, the navy had 43,070 seamen in 2019. It had only 1,584 MCPOs in that year.

CHAPTER THREE

WHAT IS DAILY LIFE LIKE IN THE NAVY?

Daily life in the US Navy is broken into shifts. Sailors spend time doing their job, standing watch, sleeping, or enjoying free time. Each person has a specific job. Everyone does his or her part to make sure missions run smoothly. A successful ship requires teamwork.

Sailors take a test aboard the aircraft carrier
USS **Nimitz.**

The space on a navy ship is limited.

But the ship's crew still gets a variety of

experiences. Sailors learn and train while

on board their ship. College professors

sometimes teach on ships. They might

teach sailors college-level courses. Or they

might teach sailors new languages. Sailors

sometimes do missions on shore.

Rear Admiral Cedric Pringle leads the

National War College. This is a university

in Washington, DC. Pringle is an officer

DRESS CODES

Navy sailors have to follow certain dress codes. Men's hair must be less than 2 inches (5 cm) long. Women's hair has to be no more than 3 inches (8 cm) below their uniform collar. If their hair is longer, it must be pulled back from their face. Sailors cannot have extreme body art or piercings. They cannot have tattoos on their head. They can have very small neck tattoos. Their tattoos must not show through white clothes.

who served as an engineer in the navy.

He helped with disaster relief missions. He

says, "There are people who are tasked

to do different things . . . but we all come

together for a common vision."[6]

Sailors put in long days of hard work. But

living on a ship can be enjoyable too. Sailors

have some free time. There are gyms on

navy ships. Sailors may work out. They

might play card games or watch movies.

WHERE DO SAILORS LIVE?

There are different living areas on board

navy ships. Each sailor has a bed and a

place to store personal items. Ships also

have a kitchen, dining hall, and lounge area. Many ships have internet and mail services too. These services help sailors stay connected to loved ones back home.

When sailors are not at sea, they live on a base. A base is a community that looks like a neighborhood. Bases are designed to meet sailors' needs. They have stores and movie theaters. They also have churches, libraries, and fitness centers.

Sailors who are single can live in an apartment or a barracks. A barracks is a large building. It has many rooms. Sailors live together in a barracks. Other sailors

*Sailors relax in a lounge on the USS **Kitty Hawk**.*

live on base with their families. They have

more housing options. They can live in their

own houses. Some homes have garages,

Naval bases have spaces for the navy's ships to dock.

porches, or big yards. Living spaces on

base have many of the same comforts as

civilian homes. They have full kitchens and

laundry machines.

CONTINUING EDUCATION

Some sailors may not have a college

degree. They may want to earn a degree

later on. The US Navy has a special program to help them. It is called the Navy College Program. Sailors can get academic credits for the training and work they do. These credits count toward their degree. Sailors may study on ships and submarines in their spare time. They may also have time to take classes while serving in another country. The program counts these classes as credits too.

The US Navy also offers a tuition assistance program. It pays for up to 100 percent of a sailor's education. Sailors can use this money to pay for college-level

College fairs aboard US Navy ships help sailors learn about educational opportunities.

classes. They must take these classes on

their own time, not while they are serving.

People sometimes borrow money to pay

for their education. This borrowed money is

called a loan. People must pay this money

back. The navy helps service members and

veterans pay off their loans.

THE NAVAL POSTGRADUATE SCHOOL

Navy service members or veterans can go

to the Naval Postgraduate School (NPS).

This school is in Monterey, California.

The NPS helps people get master's and

doctorate degrees. It offers degrees

in business and engineering. Students

can also get degrees in science and

international studies. Other specialty

NPS programs include health care, law,

and religion.

The navy needs intelligent and skilled people. It encourages people to continue their education. Lieutenant Erick Samayoa is a naval officer. He went to the NPS. The navy chose him for a special science and engineering program. He was one of only a few officers chosen. He said,

HONORING SERVICE MEMBERS

The US military awards medals to honor service members. Heath Robinson received eight medals throughout his career. He served in the navy from 1997 to 2011. He worked as a sailor for a few years. Then he became a Navy SEAL. Robinson died while he was deployed in Afghanistan. Five of his medals have a "V" on them. This "V" stands for valor. The medals recognize his courage in combat.

"[This] program gives us the opportunity to pursue research projects that will help bring promising technology to the **fleet**."[7]

CHAPTER FOUR

WHERE DO SAILORS SERVE?

Sailors are usually assigned to a ship for three years. They do not spend all of this time at sea. Most ships are docked at their home **port** for long periods of time. Sailors may be out at sea for six to nine months at a time.

After serving on a ship, most sailors are assigned to serve three years on shore.

Sailors are often on their ships for months at a time.

They work on a naval base. Sailors may

serve in the United States. Or they may

serve at a US naval base in another country.

In 2019, some deployments took sailors

to the Middle East. Other sailors went to

Canada or Iceland. These are just some of

the many places where sailors might work.

In the United States, sailors commonly

serve along the coast. Virginia and Florida are the states with the most naval bases.

TRAVEL AND DEPLOYMENT

Travel is a daily part of working aboard a ship. Sometimes ships stop at foreign ports. They drop off or pick up supplies. Sailors may have a chance to go into town. They can experience other parts of the world.

THE LARGEST NAVIES

The US Navy has the world's largest, most powerful ships. It also employs the most people. About 432,000 people worked for the US Navy in 2019. The US Navy had 288 ships in 2019. China's navy had a larger number of ships. However, they were mostly smaller and less capable than their US counterparts.

Mass communications specialists take photos of life aboard the ship.

Navy ships commonly go to Japan. They also go to Italy and other parts of Europe.

A service member's experience while abroad depends on her job. Not all people are involved in combat. For example, some are mass communications specialists (MCs). MCs are journalists. They take photos and videos. They travel with navy sailors. They tell sailors' stories. They may update the navy's social media. One MC says, "The ship is always moving through the water. Something is always happening. . . . There [are] about 2,500 people on board, and that's 2,500 different stories."[8]

MISSIONS

Sailors may be deployed for many reasons. Some help people in other countries. Lieutenant Junior Grade Kimberly Herm was deployed in Afghanistan in 2012. She was a civil engineer. She helped build schools, roads, and bridges. Sometimes

Lieutenant Junior Grade Kimberly Herm (left) worked with local people when she served in Afghanistan.

she worked at a school while students were

in class. Young girls were often afraid of

US service members. So the girls hid from

them. Herm helped comfort them. She said,

I would take off my helmet and sunglasses so they could see I was a girl too. Their reaction would immediately change. . . . I have always hoped that my presence there . . . had a positive impact on these young girls.[9]

WHAT DO SAILORS DO IN THEIR FREE TIME?

Fitness is important in the navy. Sailors must always be ready to respond to an emergency. They need to stay in good shape. Naval bases have workout centers. Sailors can participate in softball leagues,

Members of the navy deployed to Afghanistan play basketball on their base.

basketball tournaments, and yoga. The

navy also has youth programs for sailors'

children. Some programs offer childcare

for young kids. Others focus on youth

entertainment. Kids can join sports. They may do arts and crafts.

A special navy program helps sailors find entertainment. It is called Information, Tickets & Tours (ITT). Sailors can go to movies, concerts, zoos, and theme parks. ITT helps them find options in the United

WHAT DO SAILORS CALL PARTS OF A SHIP?

Sailors call parts of a ship certain names. They use these names to communicate with each other. Sailors call the floor the *deck*. The eating area is the *mess deck*. A bathroom is a *head*. A kitchen is a *galley*. Some names make directions clear. For example, the *stern* is the back of the ship. The *bow* is the front of the ship. Instead of "going downstairs," a sailor would say he is "going below."

A group of sailors arrive at the Singapore Zoo while their ship is docked in the city.

States and in foreign countries. Sailors

can watch movies while aboard ships. The

navy has its own movie service. Sailors can

choose from more than 500,000 videos.

Across the globe, members of the US Navy are ready to defend the United States at sea.

Sailors get up to thirty paid vacation days each year. They can spend them any way they want. Many sailors use this time to visit family. They may also go on a trip.

Life in the US Navy is different for each person. Navy service members use their skills to help others. They learn valuable lessons in commitment and service. The US Navy is a great career path for many people.

GLOSSARY

civilians

people who are not part of a country's military

deployed

sent away from a home base on a military mission

fleet

a group of ships that are under the command of one officer

hostages

people who are held prisoner by an enemy during a war

missiles

explosive weapons that can strike far away

oath

a set of rules or ideas someone promises to follow

ordnance

military supplies such as weapons, tools, or vehicles

port

a town or city with a harbor where ships are kept

veterans

people who served in the military

SOURCE NOTES

INTRODUCTION: DEFENDING THE COUNTRY

1. Quoted in "Stuntwoman," *US Navy*, n.d. www.navy.com.

CHAPTER ONE: HOW DO PEOPLE JOIN THE NAVY?

2. Quoted in "The Achiever," *US Navy*, n.d. www.navy.com.

3. Quoted in "Navy Chaplain Careers," *US Navy*, n.d. www.navy.com.

CHAPTER TWO: WHAT JOBS ARE AVAILABLE?

4. Quoted in "Lifeline," *US Navy*, n.d. www.navy.com.

5. Quoted in "Navy Diver Careers," *US Navy*, n.d. www.navy.com.

CHAPTER THREE: WHAT IS DAILY LIFE LIKE IN THE NAVY?

6. Quoted in "Life as a Sailor," *US Navy*, n.d. www.navy.com.

7. Quoted in Tom Tonthat, "NPS Initiates Meyer Scholar Program to Develop Air and Missile Defense Experts," *Naval Postgraduate School*, n.d. www.nps.edu.

CHAPTER FOUR: WHERE DO SAILORS SERVE?

8. Quoted in "Mass Communication Specialist Careers," *US Navy*, n.d. www.navy.com.

9. Quoted in Lauren Katzenberg, "40 Stories from Women about Life in the Military," *New York Times Magazine*, March 8, 2019. www.nytimes.com.

FOR FURTHER RESEARCH

BOOKS

Roberta Baxter, *Work in the Military*. San Diego, CA: ReferencePoint Press, 2020.

Sarah Crickard, *John Paul Jones and the Birth of the American Navy*. New York: PowerKids Press, 2016.

Nancy Miller, *My Mom Is in the Navy*. New York: PowerKids Press, 2016.

Chris Oxlade, *Inside Battleships*. Minneapolis, MN: Lerner Publishing Group, 2017.

INTERNET SOURCES

"Explore Navy Careers," *US Navy*, n.d. www.navy.com.

"Steps for Admission," *United States Naval Academy*, n.d. www.usna.edu.

"What to Expect at Navy Boot Camp," *Military.com*, 2020. www.military.com.

WEBSITES

Naval Special Warfare
www.sealswcc.com

This website explains how people can become Navy SEALs. It also provides tips for getting in shape.

The Navy SEAL Museum
www.navysealmuseum.org

The Navy SEAL Museum is in Fort Pierce, Florida. It shares the history of the US Navy SEALs.

The US Navy
www.navy.com

The US Navy website gives information about different navy jobs. It also explains the enlistment process.

INDEX

IMAGE CREDITS

ABOUT THE AUTHOR

Emma Huddleston lives in the Twin Cities with her husband. She enjoys writing children's books and staying active. She is thankful for all who serve in the US military and make the world a safer place.